Strongin's language is muscular, challenging, disarming, and utterly unexpected as she journeys through childhood illness to the demands of age, circling, looking back, returning always to the body's insistent desires: *The need roughens in me to have love. The way the paper has tooth.* I have never read anything like it.

—RACHEL ROSE, Poet Laureate, Vancouver, BC

Lynn Strongin is a force of nature.

—CHASE TWICHELL, Winner of the 2011 Kingsley Tufts Award

Fascinating work.

—ALICIA OSTRIKER, Chancellor of the Academy of American Poets

Lynn Strongin has written a book that reintroduces us to ourselves, to the naked spirit of ourselves, and this accomplishment is very rare. In the shadow of her words, a cold wind kicks up. Then slowly, deftly, she weaves a 25-part hymn to steadfastness and grace, to a lifetime of physical deprivation, spiritual yearning and barely held-back exultation in each sensory gift. Each poem in *Burn* leaves its imprint, its scald-mark, on us.

—CHARLES ADÈS FISHMAN, Winner of the 2012 New Millennium Award for Poetry & the 2014 Aesthetica Creative Writing Award for Poetry

Strongin puts the verve back into verse. The acuity with which her older woman narrator investigates life is rare and invigorating.

—BETSY WARLAND, Author of *Breathing the Page: Reading the Act of Writing*

Selected Titles by Lynn Strongin

The Dwarf Cycle (1972)

Paschal Poem: Now in the Green Year's Turning (1976)

Toccata of the Disturbed Child (1977)

Countrywoman/Surgeon (1979)

The Sorrow Psalms: A Book of Twentieth-Century Elegy (ed.) (2006)

Albino Peacock (2008)

Spectral Freedom, Selected Poetry, Criticism, and Prose (2009)

Twin Tan Dogs, Obedience & Discipline (2010)

Dark Salt: A Brush with Genius (2011)

Orphan Thorns (2012)

Bread of the Angels (2012)

The Burn Poems

The Burn Poems

Lynn Strongin

HEADMISTRESS PRESS

ISBN-13: 978-0692370940
ISBN-10: 0692370943

Cover art © 2003 MADY ART (Marie Bourdages). *Baleine en Putréfaction, Série Mémoires de Baleines,* 28 x 34 pouces, huile sur toile.

Cover & book design by Mary Meriam

PUBLISHER
Headmistress Press
60 Shipview Lane
Sequim, WA 98382
Telephone: 917-428-8312
Email: headmistresspress@gmail.com
Website: headmistresspress.blogspot.com

For Penelope Weiss

Contents

THE TENDERNESS OF THE WREN

The heart it gives us when the beloved gets well.

The sunken anchor thru the blue of despond when they fail to heal.

Some days

Patterning walls

With rood mice church mice asters takes all the breath one has like blowing out a candle when on a lung machine.

I slept beside the Iron one, the lung

Not breathless yet but nearly won

Over to the other side.

I had a terror so I sang

Under my breath

Over & under swam

The blue fish of eternity. My miniature nurse with the toe bunion is worse: it weeps.

Love keeps.

With the tender telling of small things

The imprint of song

In embryo or full-blown. Hair like corn silk. Like milk.

The dignity we must accord each other.

Glacial, from Iceland, comes the wind.

Warm-hearted laughing comes the girl from Ireland.

When she slips from me and I agonize

I REMIND MYSELF IT IS ONLY THE LLAMA IN HER

Quiet manners

Like when I go thru the wall & over the roof

Under the barn

Still I am the infant-bard having drawn a brute hand:

Jack of lanterns, all spades

Digging children's open graves

Those bigheads staring up at eternity

Thin lips in mockery of a lipsticked smile

Rouged cheeks

Which the mortician's esthetician has applied.

The need roughens in me to have love. The way the paper has tooth.

But when I say I'm glad you're back in town

Be my valentine

The sob is in the glottal stop.

Do go skiing

Take my legs with you

Gravest nurse of all

My muse most enlightened by you

I drape rope pearls about your neck.

You give me a shoulder rub, which excites me, & I blush but you
stand behind.

Rope pearls aside, I will cook you no sacrificial lamb

But the thin one the trinity we allow the tallow

THE BARN OWL HAVING FLOWN OVER

The winter sunset mellow

For you, the tenderness we extend wounded things, the attention to detail

The tenderness for small things:

Your passport having expired two months

Ought to have been given ministerial reprieve

Compassionate reprieve

Such as I was given when I flew the coop of heaven

For this northern post my haven

Of new dark & wintry silks:

Nay! Not for gin (we drank too much)

Nor for beating about the flat in moth-eaten sweaters

But for deep down

In the gut

Between the legs

That ski & ride

Pelvic passion:

The purest Sapphic Ode ever

Given.

Val & Angel at the nightfall of the world

Stage backdrop behind them unfurled

One had given the other burgundy pearls

Quarrels or no more quarrels?

Corn dolls or no more corn dolls?

Babies or real babies?

Do you wait for share hour because you are tired of me?

As the eyes tire of reading a much-loved book once

Put aside forever or for the once.

In all events

It makes me want to curl up in a ball & die

But be found still berthing

By the barn

With a blue-gold eye

Wrapped in gold old cloth

With pity, suicidal sorrow, our years of

Colors that blind sight the eye.

I THOUGHT YOU WERE TIRED OF ME, SWEET GEORGIA BROWN

As one tires of field upon field of radiant corn.

The sound of the john bowl flushing

The flushed-from-bush ptarmigan

Had more interest, was more keen than one more birthday.

Who wanted to be seventy-seven? After all

The abacus adds up numbers,

One forgets to blot the lips at table

To taste the sweet wine going down.

O bring me the towel warmed

To wrap my nightgown in after surgery

Even though minor surgery

It cleft to the heart thru sternum, the wound.

After the year in hell

I think we can look ahead to the time when, with ungloved hand we
lift the injured

Wren in both hands cupped:

When I was a child, I drank a cup of cinders.

Swirl of ashes against the prison sky & walls: brick.

Now doctor, my seventy-fifth year, wouldn't thou send me to another
island for detoxification.

I touch leather. I knock wood.

I looked up at the sky-ceiling imagining it the Sistine

WHERE CHILDREN RAN WHEELCHAIR RACES IN A SPECIAL OLYMPICS

That was forecast of what was to come, has come.

Lower the sorrow, Levinson.

She had that shine of a crossroads

Where five rivers meet

Each mirroring a different globe.

Lullaby, Glory.

Till, folded arms like a crane across sweltered chest

Scant breast

Later I learned the double mastectomy had left no breast.

The sweaters the tunics she wore a kaleidoscope of all colors.

My jogger

But mainly Renaissance velvety hues, tints, lullaby

Toque hat of raspberry.

She was working on a Lincoln project when I met her.

She'd come on a ferryboat

& by train

& bus

alchemies of transport led her to my side

my supple-wristed

cross-laced

northern bride.

BUT HER LACES WERE LEATHERS

Weathered the finest in the family of leathers.

Earth boots

Solid feet surefooted as a mountain goat

Thick socks folded back.

She had no lack

(I have a half sister with assessed property value two mil

I need a new brace for my back).

The lion will teach us bravery

The eagle to be imperious

The lamb to be meek.

I choose the lamb: my beloved, pale as white ash rests in the next room

Propped on dreams:

The dream of us like the poet born in Pickwick, Dam Hardin County, Tennessee

Growing up among Blue Mountains.

The Army intelligence is stain

We have none of.

We translate sounds:

The gong into the Autoharp. The flute into the pennywhistle:

For self-defense, we hold what sword?

Landscape? Technique?

Born rescuers steal in silence to the sickbed: born helpers.

Nightshades make me look a small Amelia Earhart

I could not shield myself against paralysis however hard

I tried. The ghost that ran over my little world

Multiplied

In meanings

Burned, then scarred:

No change of love. No change of Lord.

I did not know how to live our lives any other way

Than straw upon snow:

I abhorred asphalt.

Choosing rather a twofold field: one half ivory snows the other blond straw:

Yes it evoked the medieval world.

Words were hurled for lances.

We did olden dances.

The two fields resembled a boy's hair

Parted straight down the middle:

One of those Middle Ages haircuts that was in some years ago.

Now part of the past

However the image may last:

Blond was youth

White-silver age

Against however we rage

Advances

Turning page-by-page

Tell tears dim water meadows

Melt snow

Hand-in-hand though in separate rooms

Divided by illness

We swim thru fire

We reach out our hands thru walls to hold the other's fine-boned delicate

Lard hand.

How I worried yesterday when she was late

Why rage against fate?

Fate is simply what happens.

Nothing to hate.

Yet I set the cordless phone on the back of the toilet tank

I lit the votive candle on the edge of the tub

I sank into childhood deeper & deeper

Until I understood—it dawned on me

Fully

Like a reckoning, first slowly now totally

It was after all her in earth boots,

Cheeks flushed to a child out of a nineteenth-century storybook

Collar high like a boy out of John Donne morning

O schoolboy

Time & work have wrought all they could against joy

BUT THE MUSCLED FISTS OF DESTROY

Win no hearts.

There is music only in

Gaudate. Ex Maria.

Exultate. Long ago, in the Hebrides, I caught her filmic silhouette, tapered fine hand

Holding cigarette to lip.

Beyond, yet what language lulls God

The Saturday morning station in the South

The wrong notes of the school child

Imagination's wildest benders

All contain it:

The whitest snow,

The plow-turned, human-trod sod.

When even the rag doll looks corpsy

You looked limp when we woke up today.

We never got up:

On whose eyes would be put the penny?

(On the other side of the continent, ice storm)

It's only the other side of death—

Exhaustion:

Trembling, at the edge, toying with the idea of getting in touch with
a half sister

Dangerous toy

Radioactive like rooms in Hospital

I must don an apron.

Noon comes soup.

Late noon my Zhivago coat of rest:

In its length, in its furs

I see Mrs Pouffy

Now no corpsy rag doll

But bending as flowers bend, her signature blown in smoke

Flexible in thunderstorms, which pass on by

Branches lending a face in the winter night:

Exhaustion wheeled to the toy box & healed

The Zhivago coat covers our toes, the lining shelters us we keep sinking

Made do & mended

By sleep on sleep on sleep:

Zhivago hours

Prayers said in a time of sickness

Swept over me till I buttoned my Zhivago coat up to my chin.

RECURRENCE

When it strikes at first I flick my wax candle on

Then slip the Amelia Earhart Nightshade on

Either over my hand or under my chin till both green eyes are blinking:

Only lashes sweep the imitation velvet lining.

Does she know precisely when she starts wounding me?

When dishwater powder makes her curse I sprinkle some on the floor.

When frowns sweep off smiles

Dark weather coming.

There was a silversmith, a woman, named Chloe Darke

The perfect name now in these hours for my beloved:

Hence while Chloe Darke sweeps my mess

I close my eyes night will come night will bless dogs

And woo us

The mittened frost will batten windows

Of isinglass.

But all is not peace in the dollhouse.

Springs forth the rat behind the wall

Retreats the mouse

The mouse among the precious of this earth

Like ibis

Like sapphire

Like man-o-war blue to an extreme that woos us

But when we touch we must have all the dignity we allow the barn owl

& the titmouse.

O lord of all creatures scuttling from fires, from curse

And worse.

Is it either eat or be eaten?

Our fathers taught us cold grace

Sitting in their harp-back chairs

Making a solemn music

Giving us children to know greater than speech

We silent voice our love.

So we bowed to the voice we could not hear:

In our long johns, in our nightdress

While the dogs barking outside had still to be fed.

Soon it was bed

The tulip flare of sheets fresh ironed

Being turned back by mother

We zipped into the dark cups of sleep.

A RELIQUARY EVENING FOR SURE

The bones in their tiny boxes, rosettes under glass.
—Charles Wright, "Last Supper," from *The Wrong End of the Rainbow*

Nostalgia is an apron

I want her true

I want her home

I want her deep down.

The down of the owl feathering for night each pinion in order like a letter on a printer's tray.

I want her to stay

Close

Not paralyzed like me

But content in her apron of photography: printed, filmic security

The image holy holy holy.

Bliss comes like flare of lit match

And can be blown out as quickly:

By word

Or gesture of spoon shaken in a nod of the preacher making the spoon nod.

Is the Wrong End of the Rainbow the one with no pot of gold?

Darkness closes in—

It cannot be my imagining

The day before she

My loved she-bird must go back to work: Let's proceed carefully. Not
lay the fairytale book away.

Office behavior, the stacking the things

My stacking of hopes sliding.

Maybe she loved me—for all the labor

As her sick child

Who had to be positioned a certain way:

Two hot water bottles: one on the lumbar spine, one higher

And icepack on the popo,

Maybe patching me was holy.

Now dashing away

Flashing

Butterflies under glass like pheasant under glass.

Winter has its own cutlery.

God knows during these days sick home became

Cooking soups

Polishing cutlery

Propping pillows: a cubicle of curing every corner of day

Like mail slots in old hotels

Like pushing into darkness & the back

Of the medicine cab all that came over the months & years from the local pharmacy.

Help us to hold fast to what makes us button the top button of the cape most tenderly.

That it cover all of thee. Of me.

Zhivago coat

Feel you're in a romantic movie

Furry. Fun Fabulous. Over the top. Go for it.

We hinder down under

Moles in earth beavers building dam

Wrens nesting.

Our Zhivago coat of memories, nonetheless, is besting.

Reality: harsh fact today

Narrative's a chiaroscuro country

The lyric, light-shot, we have left behind

Which tells us our stories

Giving them beginning and end.

Lord of Hard trips in unkind weather

Take down our memories, our notes

The thaw will come of winter

Help us over the ice

Guide us, holding hands, handing hard to what was near

Us once: Ecstasy,

Barley Creek. A farewell to Appalachia, a handshake with New England

A bled off having come to the end of something:

My miniature nurse with bunion worse for all her passion to do so many, too many things

That now the source and steam of the wound in recurring cold is weeping.

GOD'S RUMMAGE SALE: RAGS & BONES!

Rags & bones! went the voice.

A cross between an elf & a sparrow

Caroled & crystalline

Sweet & salt

Waiting waiting without halt

Like the body

Haltered

By hope & despair

Crossing the Rubicon

Touching shore

Almost here when it crumbles into thin air.

O my God my angels why have you become beyond despair?

I cannot tell the beloved

The beast in the greenery

Nobody near

So bending my ear

To earth of leather

I harness

The cry meant to be shouted clear

Clearly

Clearest

To the rummage sale

Repair

Federal & provincial no longer made of bone, breath, and hair.

The dollhouse is at peace

All the little windows of the soul

Closed moon shines on the toys

The ease with which cavil took place

Something slowly learned like climbing a ladder.

Nothing to have a bird over, one learns in great age

Which, in youth, was brute anger provoking.

At ease

The mother climbs the stairs to bed

"Sleepyhead," she tousles her small son,

kisses her daughter.

The small world of the dollhouse, the miniature globe

Of *The Wind in the Willows* on the bedside table

Is at peace.

The cold less cruel than back at Yule

When it shot the human heart

It shut the schools.

It is only the little creatures that scuttle to & fro

Who kick up a wind

A wind so small that birds in their little arks the darkest day of the year

Huddle near.

Only the human heart rocks, throws out a clear beam of fear.

How far has the railroad train travelled in the dollhouse?

I refer to one single morning's journey.

Peace in the dollhouse

After the wounds of war

My big braw girl goes out to straddle the world

I leap hurdles at home

ALL THE PANES BE FOGGED OVER TO PEARL

The child weeps under the apple tree. Why? While the winter
woodsman chops the blue water to blue lumber

All the panes are smeared with pearl

It is he who is cruel

The beautiful so close to us

As hipbone rubbing against bone: a new one must be set in

Her time of anguish is round the bend.

The winter wood fills a pewter mug with slate blue

Slate enough to bold a home true.

Carpenter truer the beam with spirit bulb,

Old workhorse, shire & the kine are red with wintering, rouge as
October apple red New England brick schools

I go in my orange coat among

Them walking to the far away place the unicorn:

Lincoln's dug her? Lincoln's son?

Long-legged long-spirited

Had held:

The sky and pewter pitcher

Blue blue and heart breaking

Breath taking hue

Cobalt

Are the wedding bands

Of Abe & me

True.

The Ruckus is done.

Of Holland, the orangerie

I see monks in a monastery

Bent black cowls barely move against ivory

The pain in my spine's bedded down.

O dollie. Mrs Pouffy.

Wood chop waves of Holland

Rehearse

Restate

Reshape the Jewish mystic

But do not

Excuse those who injected the blue numerals under the skin.

I lay a blond head on a wood arm: pile of cloud stone counting the little windows of the small shattered slanted, stunned in silence till we come round with words which urge us love him again.

My hands are tied. I am paralyzed.

Is that eidetic sound image, or hallucinogen I hear in the inmost imitating drum?

Dutch doors

One half, bottom swung open to slagheap of ashes, which like water swirls

At the stir of the hand or a southern small wind.

The top half reveals: ocean, azures like the skies.

Lower is the great hospital, hospice for germinal pain to which one wheels, a child being wheeled again and again

A broken record.

The upper a brand new shining visit by Dali, Salvador: the ocean

Lines, lens of Dutch doors click, like cameras click open: we have limitless passions:

Child with neck brace, candlewick thin & bright.

The Dutch door's upper half closes upon wood-carved waves:

Pewter of lamplight moonshines on its hinges:

Perfectly docketed.

All your needs all my needs under sky half-met

We embrace

Tea to blot like ink from the eye

Diurnal time is scrolled:

Among the great-unwashed sun will rise again

which sinks now upon all

those who live it up, those who wish to die: the waves of sleep inscrolled a
blanket over them of heaven blue-grey.
Peek thru the top half to the lower

God's chickens peck at crystal fodder, gold to orange fish smaller & smaller

Like boys receding becoming smaller & smaller

My waking slow, living in city in town so small. . .

Clouded by February longings…year past. . .that coming.

The ashes of the Rubicon swirl

Mastheads loom ahead: they too are minuscule:

Where am I to cross to? What faraway place, and on what journey?

Small house in small village emotions billow, blown silk like flame out windows

Reflecting back in windowpanes:

The whole dollhouse is at peace

But all the little windows of the soul

Are out blown by conflagration:

I am the peace of Holocaust, inferno see all the little men & women & the
children burn.

WHEN NIGHT COMES DOWN ON NOWHERE VILLE

All the little windows of the soul

Light up

Where life is swung like the Dutch door

Open upon morning's roar

Of children

At nightfall

All the windows, shuttered with a purple cast

Are lit

Whale oil ignited lamps for sailors' wives

And when they were widowed

Their own pole-

Vaulting began

Of grief

Into a meadow iridescent:

Now is night: All the brightest windows of soul

Burn burn open the disk Moon shines

Upon the bubbles still in the tub where the poet read of Abe Lincoln he loved to laugh:

Until I being an image-chooser, choose the vivid ones:

Furnace, boiler is shut down

And only coal

Catches moonlight the level low in the pond: a frond of fern leaves a signature in perfect schoolroom copperplate.

For those who are sad it is not too late,

Brimming with blackness

Not with bleak: on Bliss Point Avenue, the lighthouse whirls its red lantern: this is land's end.

But Coal

As deep a blue as the recesses

Of all

Extras, Jubilate, O child who needs the spinal audile in age due to the virus that swept the century's children: like ash.

Now a sash of brilliance burns about her waist

She sings a *Liberal* cautiously as in Labor's painting she bears before her, her candle.

Has trouble broken out in the dollhouse now?

To unseam a scar?

Is it weeping?

It is hard visualizing how to get to a far-off place

Reading about far-off places is different.

We separate and we are anxious

Far off place   far off place   come near:

There is fear when Vancouver Island Health Authority

Fails to send me the right helper.

I can hear ocean roaring in one ear: there is fear.

But in the other eternal peace makes its music

Children sing *Libera* and *Requiem* here.

I lie on my back visualize the Dutch door:

O to the tulip, to drink color from, then set it right in its glass stick, its home.

The half-hinged door I can cause to close

Enfolding me in a Zhivago coat warm as a mother's hug, scented as the old rose.

All warmth no far-away places here:

Instead all the small windows of the soul are lit and burning warmth, which cannot ever

Tip extremes to flame: I am called. I waken to answer. I know my name.

Rummaging thru boxes of old laces

Ruminating in a scrum love & anger combined:

Soot-grey, ink-black. Thunder-color: thews of love & anger: boots'
ring, shoelaces

Braces were stropped, not high black little old lady shoes:

I came upon the series of ancient orthopedic braces: for leg, for back,
for neck.

The moon was at a stasis:

Burning above one candle for love, one for ecstasies

Turned back upon when youth ended.

We had it so good.

Teddy, who would want a paralytic infant?

It started up again: in seventy-forth year it kicked back at me the boar

With bristle of wild pig and more sting.

It was an everlasting thing.

Don't call it by its name. Word magic then?

Don't look at it in a mirror doubled.

Don't use the word said friends

My nearest dearest:

Rummaging among cartons of old dress laces

Ecru, blue, elite I found one with a child engraved in string

By fingers cut off at the second joint

With dirty string:

It wanted to have the shape of a heart

But ended

In the shape of a steeple

Collapsing:

I stroked it in both hands, upped, a bird on the wing

Who had smashed into a window one foggy night

Long ago

A hundred years

In the past century:

And that's the end of the burning

Century, the unsung carol, the not mentioned, abided bone-deep pain.

In all the dollhouse, pillaged, I could not find the brace

That would lock me forever in place.

The dollhouse has ended up as pure toast, melted to wax

After the fire last night—I should have known.

I would have said it was the saddest bake, our love nearly burned to the ground

But here it is—

Not quite itself

But back again:

Tragedy staring at itself smiling back in a pond.

I told you the wicks were wicked when I woke & knew we could not go on

I saw the pain redoubled at lunch sought *Crystal Dragon*

From our past suddenly saw myself an old woman

But penny-bright

Sharp-penned

In the *Icelandic Images* store where you bought me on impulse the sweater scratchy

Only as the dragonfly of memory

On the pond of our joy.

O I lie down at the words "Paid" on a bill

Knowing like Abe Lincoln

I paid my bushel of apples to melancholy

Deserved the Goliath of immeasurable reward

Not the dollhouse-measure of David's song

Which won the gold all along a long.

Were those sorrowful times

Back on Cook Street?

Did it all melt down to kitchen?

That galley that hung

Me with gin?

Why should those times be more sorrowful than these? Ruined cities
always were in my spine:

Fort Mason. For Saint John. Fort Spaceman.

To a child it was cruel. To be a woman? There are no words:

Instead I trap

Momentarily

Cup a bird in hand

And let my tears bathe him.

FATHER OLD, OLDER LOOKING LIKE THE LITTLE PRINCE IN AN EASY CHAIR

At near eighty

O listener after the capitulation

Hitler had Warsaw leveled:

The city's existence today feels like a miracle.

Shovel ready, brown-dog scoundrels represent life in Michigan

The hacked-up nature gave it much beauty

But this sobriquet masks questionable origins.

Lo, Flyover lives live on. Our Hudson Valley Home hid the crippling
of the lives, complex that lay beneath

Like hair under a fur hat.

O we were exceptional people with exceptional lives

But Oxford, the initials of greatness, were always near

A bit of rapture caught in him & me.

Tiger, you caught me by the tail

Now things pale

In the telling.

The storyline, its Kokab shaky as a one-year old;

But it is my only way of doing things

A skipping boat calmly, right hand steady on the tiller

Thoughts in agitation.

I am close to you but I peer out at the vast dark sea

Pointing with my index finger

At total fear.

The Rubicon. The faraway.

Do you hear my footfall?

It comes from before our sorrowing days.

Across the hallways and valleys the voice carries

That holds the jug of mercies, betrayals promises

Up to the brim:

Water reflective always.

And now she gives me a clue that she loves me

& all's calm:

Alabama reflected in water,

The pillowslips ironed.

Only the sudden bolt of lightning

In the darkening southern night is frightening

As bleakness suddenly without sound brightening.

Standing at the ironing board

Or sitting in the rocking chair her tallness overwhelms me

Like Eleanor Roosevelt.

But her teeth are even although with a gap.

O rocking horse love we are given too short a time to love

Although it be a gumdrop a clothesline length

Too snapped in half

Although it be a lifeline.

UNQUESTIONABLY

They put us over barrels to burn our spines

Into arrows in the curved positions. Scoliosis not dementia

But driven to temperature above lone Fahrenheit Celsius what could a
child do but feel the flesh in layers like birch bark peel from him, her

Drive me with a stake

Hang me by a gallows

Of song

But do not try to remake me

That would take too long

A wrong

Indictment as the prelate's arm.

Lynn Strongin at 32 © 1971 Christa Fleischmann

About the Author

Born in New York City into a middle-class Jewish family, Lynn Strongin contracted polio at age 12 and was confined to the New York State Rehabilitation Center for 6 months; then continued her education through the city's homeschooling program. Following high school, she attended the Manhattan School of Music; received a degree in literature from Hunter College and an M.A. at Stanford University; and studied for her doctorate at the University of New Mexico.

In the 1960s, she collaborated with Denise Levertov in politically active Berkeley. She has taught, and her work has been taught, in college classrooms throughout the United States. Strongin has published more than a dozen books and her work appears in at least 30 anthologies. She is the recipient of two PEN grants, an American Association of University Women (ASUW) Fellowship, and an NEA Creative Writing Grant. *Countrywoman/Surgeon* was a candidate for the Elliston Award in 1979 and *Spectral Freedom* was nominated for a Pulitzer Prize in 2009.

In 1979, Strongin moved to Canada for what was supposed to be a short stay. She remained and currently lives in British Columbia.

"Very much the work of a true poet."
—Denise Levertov

"One thinks of Emily Dickinson more than any other poet."
—Cassandra Robison

"Lynn Strongin is the most innovative, exciting poet writing today."
—Hugh Fox

HEADMISTRESS PRESS BOOKS

Lovely - Lesléa Newman
Teeth & Teeth - Robin Reagler
How Distant the City - Freesia McKee
Shopgirls - Marissa Higgins
Riddle - Diane Fortney
When She Woke She Was an Open Field - Hilary Brown
God With Us - Amy Lauren
A Crown of Violets - Renée Vivien tr. Samantha Pious
Fireworks in the Graveyard - Joy Ladin
Social Dance - Carolyn Boll
The Force of Gratitude - Janice Gould
Spine - Sarah Caulfield
Diatribe from the Library - Farrell Greenwald Brenner
Blind Girl Grunt - Constance Merritt
Acid and Tender - Jen Rouse
Beautiful Machinery - Wendy DeGroat
Odd Mercy - Gail Thomas
The Great Scissor Hunt - Jessica K. Hylton
A Bracelet of Honeybees - Lynn Strongin
Whirlwind @ Lesbos - Risa Denenberg
The Body's Alphabet - Ann Tweedy
First name Barbie last name Doll - Maureen Bocka
Heaven to Me - Abe Louise Young
Sticky - Carter Steinmann
Tiger Laughs When You Push - Ruth Lehrer
Night Ringing - Laura Foley
Paper Cranes - Dinah Dietrich
On Loving a Saudi Girl - Carina Yun
The Burn Poems - Lynn Strongin
I Carry My Mother - Lesléa Newman
Distant Music - Joan Annsfire
The Awful Suicidal Swans - Flower Conroy
Joy Street - Laura Foley
Chiaroscuro Kisses - G.L. Morrison
The Lillian Trilogy - Mary Meriam
Lady of the Moon - Amy Lowell, Lillian Faderman, Mary Meriam
Irresistible Sonnets - ed. Mary Meriam
Lavender Review - ed. Mary Meriam

www.ingramcontent.com/pod-product-compliance
Lightning Source LLC
Chambersburg PA
CBHW060355050426

42449CB00011B/2997